P9-BYK-851

BASEBALL LEGENDS

Hank Aaron
Grover Cleveland Alexander
Ernie Banks
Johnny Bench
Yogi Berra
Roy Campanella
Roberto Clemente
Ty Cobb
Dizzy Dean
Joe DiMaggio
Bob Feller
Jimmie Foxx
Lou Gehrig
Bob Gibson
Rogers Hornsby
Reggie Jackson
Shoeless Joe Jackson
Walter Johnson
Sandy Koufax
Mickey Mantle
Christy Mathewson
Willie Mays
Stan Musial
Satchel Paige
Brooks Robinson
Frank Robinson
Jackie Robinson
Pete Rose
Babe Ruth
Nolan Ryan
Mike Schmidt
Tom Seaver
Duke Snider
Warren Spahn
Willie Stargell
Casey Stengel
Honus Wagner
Ted Williams
Carl Yastrzemski
Cy Young

CHELSEA HOUSE PUBLISHERS

NY

BASEBALL LEGENDS

CASEY STENGEL

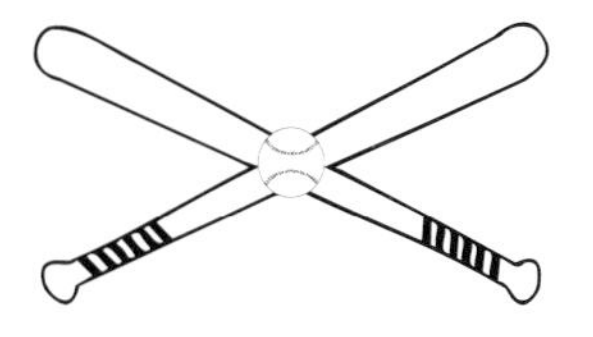

Lois P. Nicholson

Introduction by
Jim Murray

Senior Consultant
Earl Weaver

CHELSEA HOUSE PUBLISHERS
New York • Philadelphia

CHELSEA HOUSE PUBLISHERS

Editorial Director: Richard Rennert
Executive Managing Editor: Karyn Gullen Browne
Copy Chief: Robin James
Picture Editor: Adrian G. Allen
Creative Director: Robert Mitchell
Art Director: Joan Ferrigno
Manufacturing Director: Gerald Levine

Baseball Legends

Senior Editor: Philip Koslow

Staff for CASEY STENGEL

Editorial Assistant: Scott D. Briggs
Designer: M. Cambraia Magalhães
Picture Researcher: Alan Gottlieb
Cover Illustration: Daniel O'Leary

First Printing

1 3 5 7 9 8 6 4 2

Library of Congress Cataloging-in-Publication Data

Nicholson, Lois P., 1949–
Casey Stengel / Lois P. Nicholson; introduction by Jim Murray.
p. cm. (Baseball legends)
Includes bibliographical references and index.
ISBN 0-7910-2172-6
1. Stengel, Casey—Juvenile literature. 2. Baseball managers—United States—Biography Juvenile literature. [1. Stengel, Casey. 2. Baseball managers.]
I. Title. II. Series.
GV865.S8N53 1995 94-36778
796.357'092 dc20 CIP
[B] AC

CONTENTS

WHAT MAKES A STAR

Jim Murray

No one has ever been able to explain to me the mysterious alchemy that makes one man a .350 hitter and another player, more or less identical in physical makeup, hard put to hit .200. You look at an Al Kaline, who played with the Detroit Tigers from 1953 to 1974. He was pale, stringy, almost poetic-looking. He always seemed to be struggling against a bad case of mononucleosis. But with a bat in his hands, he was King Kong. During his career, he hit 399 home runs, rapped out 3,007 hits, and compiled a .297 batting average.

Form isn't the reason. The first time anybody saw Roberto Clemente step into the batter's box for the Pittsburgh Pirates, the best guess was that Clemente would be back in Double A ball in a week. He had one foot in the bucket and held his bat at an awkward angle—he looked as though he couldn't hit an outside pitch. A lot of other ballplayers may have had a better-looking stance. Yet they never led the National League in hitting in four different years, the way Clemente did.

Not every ballplayer is born with the ability to hit a curveball. Nor is exceptional hand-eye coordination the key to heavy hitting. Big-league locker rooms are filled with players who have all the attributes, save one: discipline. Every baseball man can tell you a story about a pitcher who throws a ball faster than anyone has ever seen but who has no control on or *off* the field.

The Hall of Fame is full of people who transformed themselves into great ballplayers by working at the sport, by studying the game, and making sacrifices. They're overachievers—and winners. If you want to find them, just watch the World Series. Or simply read about New York Yankee great Lou Gehrig; Ted Williams, "the Splendid Splinter" of the Boston Red Sox; or the Dodgers' strikeout king Sandy Koufax.

A pitcher *should* be able to win a lot of ballgames with a 98-miles-per-hour fastball. But what about the pitcher who wins 20 games a year with a fastball so slow that you can catch it with your teeth? Bob Feller of the Cleveland Indians got into the Hall of Fame with a blazing fastball that glowed in the dark. National League star Grover Cleveland Alexander got there with a pitch that took considerably longer to reach the plate; but when it did arrive, the pitch was exactly where Alexander wanted it to be—and the last place the batter expected it to be.

There are probably more players with exceptional ability who didn't make it to the major leagues than there are who did. A number of great hitters, bored with fielding practice, had to be dropped from their team because their home-run production didn't make up for their lapses in the field. And then there are players like Brooks Robinson of the Baltimore Orioles, who made himself into a human vacuum cleaner at third base because he knew that working hard to become an expert fielder would win him a job in the big leagues.

A star is not something that flashes through the sky. That's a comet. Or a meteor. A star is something you can steer ships by. It stays in place and gives off a steady glow; it is fixed, permanent. A star works at being a star.

And that's how you tell a star in baseball. He shows up night after night and takes pride in how brightly he shines. He's Willie Mays running so hard his hat keeps falling off; Ty Cobb sliding to stretch a single into a double; Lou Gehrig, after being fooled in his first two at-bats, belting the next pitch off the light tower because he's taken the time to study the pitcher. Stars never take themselves for granted. That's why they're stars.

1

"I WON ONE"

Manager Casey Stengel pulled his red bandanna from the pocket of his pinstriped Yankee uniform, removed the cap from his thinning crop of gray hair, and wiped his brow. Although it was cool in New York City on October 1, 1949, the tension of the final two games of the American League pennant race was enough to raise a sweat on anyone in a Yankee or Red Sox uniform that day.

New York went into the series trailing the visiting Red Sox by one game. They had to win both games to clinch the pennant. Nobody felt the pressure more than the 59-year-old Stengel. The sportswriters had laughed in amazement when the Yankees rescued Stengel from a five-year stint in the minor leagues and hired him to manage their perennial winners at the start of the season. Despite Stengel's years of baseball experience, the pundits had him pegged as a loser and a clown.

In truth, Stengel had managed nine years with the Boston Braves and the Brooklyn Dodgers in the National League and had never fin-

Manager Casey Stengel leads the New York Yankees in celebrating their pennant-clinching win over the Boston Red Sox on the final day of the 1949 season.

ished higher than fifth place. Throughout his career as a player and manager, his pranks, jokes, and stunts on and off the field had amused thousands of fans and kept many writers happily supplied with material. He could sit up all night telling and retelling his stories, embellishing and enlarging them from year to year.

Once in the minor leagues he swatted an umpire across the rear end with a bat after the ump had called him out on strikes. More than once he had captured a sparrow at the start of the game and concealed it under his cap. When he stepped up to the plate he would tip his cap, and the bird would fly out to the delight of the fans.

While everybody loved to hear about Stengel's exploits, few people believed that the Yankees—despite their obvious talent—could win with him at the helm. Surprisingly, New York opened the season strong and raced to a 12-game lead over the Red Sox in early July. But plagued with countless injuries—their greatest star, Joe DiMaggio, missed half the season—they faltered, and the Red Sox overtook them. By September, it looked as if Stengel's reputation as a loser would remain intact. However, a team that included Yogi Berra, Tommy Henrich, Phil Rizzuto, Hank Bauer, Gene Woodling, and a strong pitching staff was not about to fold. The Yankees stayed in the race as the Red Sox, led by future Hall of Famers Ted Williams and Bobby Doerr, clung to first place.

No scriptwriter could have created a more dramatic finale to a season than the weekend showdown between the traditional rivals. With 69,551 fans packing Yankee Stadium, excitement was at a fever pitch. But the Yanks were subdued when the Red Sox took an early 4–0 lead, knocking their ace, Allie Reynolds, out of the game.

When Phil Rizzuto led off in the last of the third inning, Boston's catcher, Birdie Tebbetts, made a nasty crack about the Yankees shortstop's Italian heritage. In those days, baseball players routinely traded insults, and Rizzuto took little notice of the remarks. Tebbetts then made a crucial error that never showed up in the box score. Boston had recently signed Frank Quinn, a rookie pitcher out of Yale University who had never started a big league game. "Hey Rizzuto," Tebbetts jeered, "tomorrow at this time we'll be drinking champagne, and we'll pitch the Yale kid against you guys. Think you can hit a kid from Yale, Rizzuto?"

Suddenly, fury overtook the mild-mannered Rizzuto. After grounding out, he hurled his bat away and kicked the water cooler when he returned to the dugout. Rizzuto then repeated Tebbetts's words to his teammates. The quiet

New York's Phil Rizzuto bats against the Washington Senators in the heat of the 1949 pennant race. Rizzuto—who hit a solid .275 for the year while playing 152 games at shortstop—proved to be a key factor in the Yankees' showdown with the Boston Red Sox on the final weekend of the season.

New York bench came alive with anger. Before the game, Joe DiMaggio, just recovering from a bout of viral pneumonia, had informed Stengel that he could play only three innings. But as the third inning ended, DiMaggio held up five fingers to Stengel, indicating that he would go two more. He came up in the fourth and lined a double to right that sparked a two-run rally. In the fifth, the Yankees scored two more runs to tie the game at 4–4.

Stengel kept his top reliever, Joe Page, on the mound and coolly watched the drama unfold in the most important game of his managerial career. In the bottom of the eighth, he played a hunch and let the right-handed Johnny Lindell bat against Boston right-hander Joe Dobson instead of sending up a lefty pinch hitter. Lindell laced a long home run and the Yankees led, 5–4. Page shut down Boston in the ninth, and the two rivals went into Sunday's game tied for first place.

When Vic Raschi, New York's 20-game winner, arrived at Yankee Stadium on the morning of October 2, he saw the thousands of people who had been lining up for seats since Saturday afternoon. He knew he would have to pitch the game of his life to outduel Boston's 23-game winner, Ellis Kinder. Both hurlers were hard throwers who liked to make the hitters "smell the leather," and the game promised to be a classic.

In the first inning, Rizzuto tripled and scored the first run of the game. Through seven tense innings it looked as if that was all the support Raschi would get, or all he would need. Then the Yankees broke loose in the eighth and led 5–0. In the top of the ninth the Red Sox fought back,

Joe DiMaggio heads for second base as his line drive eludes the sprawling Zeke Zarilla on October 2, 1949, the final day of the season. The Yankees and Red Sox entered the game tied for first place, and the New Yorkers' 5–3 victory earned them the first of five straight American League pennants.

scoring three runs, but finally Birdie Tebbetts popped up for the final out. The Yankees had a 5–3 win, and Stengel had finally managed a pennant-winning team in the major leagues. In the postgame bedlam of the Yankees clubhouse, the beaming New York skipper told reporters, "I want to thank all these players for giving me the greatest thrill of my life." Stengel sincerely meant those words.

Casey Stengel had dedicated himself to baseball since the day in 1910 when he broke in with the Kansas City Blues at the age of 19. He had played in three World Series, but that was long ago and forgotten. Whatever he had done as a player had become overshadowed by his years of trying—without success—to win with teams of green rookies and overripe veterans, and his ability to take the sting out of defeat by keeping everybody laughing.

In the midst of the clubhouse celebration, Stengel caught sight of his old friend Babe Herman, a former slugger who had played for the Brooklyn Dodgers and Cincinnati Reds. "Babe, I won one," Stengel exulted. "Babe, I won one. I won one."

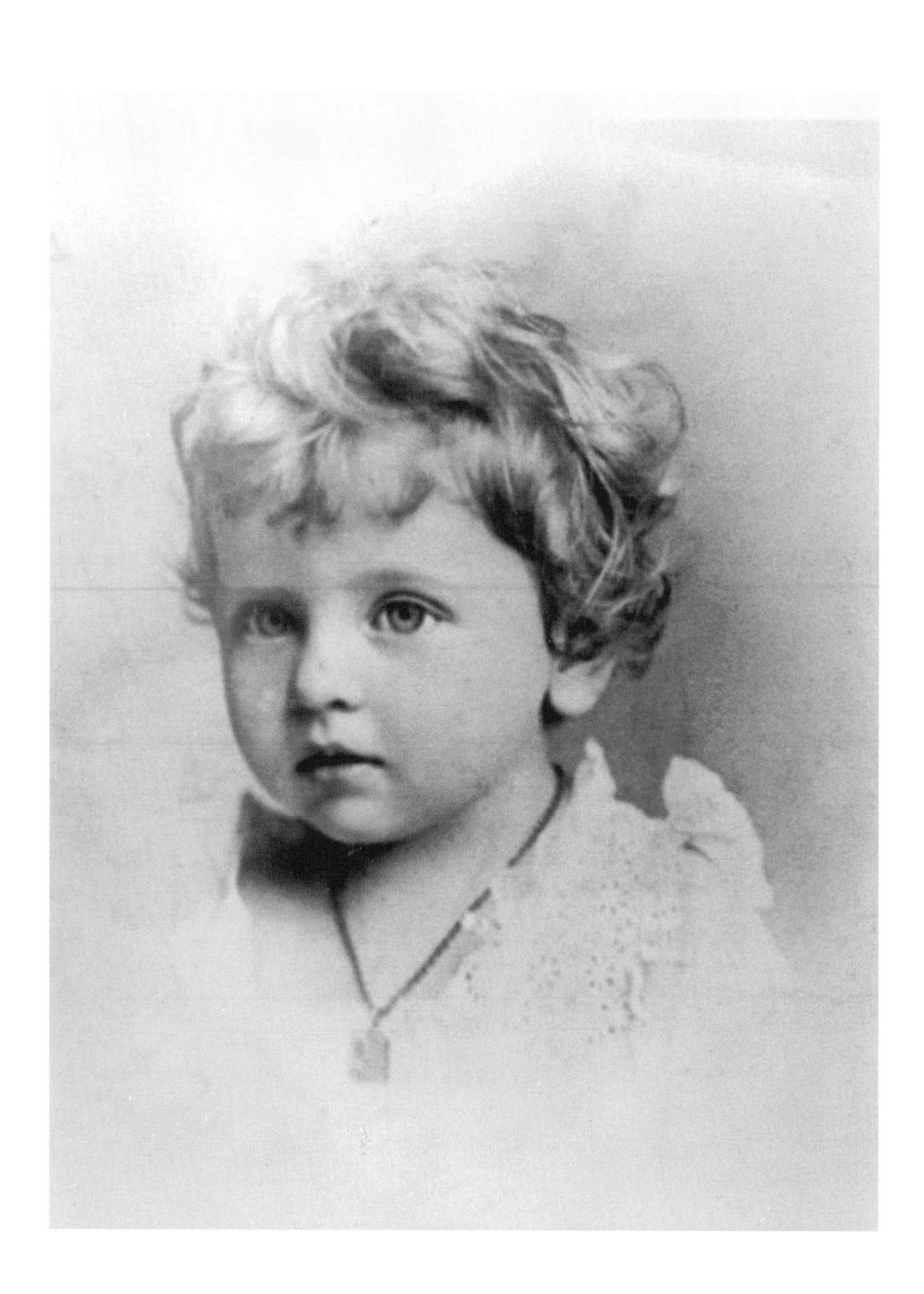

2

MISSOURI ROOTS

Charles Dillon Stengel was born on July 30, 1890, in Kansas City, Missouri. Charley, as the family called him, was the third child of Louis and Jennie Stengel. His sister, Louise, had been born in 1886, and his brother, Grant, in 1887.

Louis Stengel supported his family by working as an insurance agent; even though the Stengels were not wealthy, they enjoyed a comfortable life, renting a succession of spacious homes with large yards where the children played with their friends. Stengel's memories of his childhood centered around a warm and loving family. "The best thing I had," he remembered, "was that the family allowed everybody to come to our home. My mother always liked everyone in the neighborhood, and they could all come and use our yard." The Stengels kept chickens and a cow, enjoying fresh eggs, milk, and butter. Known for her lemon pie, Jennie Stengel was a fine cook. "We liked everything my mother cooked," said her youngest son. "She put out the best meals in the neighborhood."

Charley, always big for his age, had thick arms and legs and a barrel chest, whereas Grant was frail and slight. The two Stengel boys were inseparable, always playing cops and robbers or

Charles Dillon Stengel at the age of three. Called Charley by his family, the sturdy, high-spirited youngster began to excel at football and baseball while still in grade school.

cowboys and Indians. Their heroes were the famous outlaw brothers, Jesse and Frank James. When the Stengel brothers were not shooting it out with toy guns, they could be found playing hide-and-seek, baseball, or hockey. Their hockey sticks were rough specimens carved from tree limbs, and a crushed can served as the puck.

The arrival of snow meant sledding and the construction of elaborate snow forts. The neighborhood boys would arm themselves with snowballs, hide inside the fortress, and wait for some unsuspecting wagon driver to ride by. At the appropriate moment, they would pelt the targeted teamster with a great barrage of snowballs. Occasionally, a teamster would chase after the fleeing boys. "We'd usually get away," remembered Stengel, "but once in a while they'd catch one or two of us and beat us up."

Everyone liked Charley, but he was no student. He was naturally left-handed, and when he entered first grade, his teacher required him to write with his right hand. This practice later helped him as a ballplayer. "I stayed left-handed in throwing and hitting," he explained, "but in catching the ball I naturally had to use my right hand, and because of my penmanship I was more agile with my right hand in everything."

Charley made time for baseball between school and his chores at home, and by the age of 10, he was an excellent player. (Grant Stengel, despite his slender build, was also outstanding at the game.) The playing fields of Charley's childhood were crude by today's standards, and there was hardly any equipment. Worn balls with rips and tears were carefully repaired with friction tape until they became heavy black lumps.

Split bat handles were held together with tacks. Gloves were small, with little padding. Most boys never had decent equipment until they earned a spot on a school team.

In Charley's era, elementary school extended through grade eight, and students could finish the requirements in either January or June. Charley was 15 when he completed Garfield Grammar School in January 1906. Eleven days later, he entered Central High School. Having grown to 5 feet 8 and 170 pounds, he excelled at football as well as baseball. He became known as Dutch, a common nickname for young men of German heritage.

There was no radio or television in those days. It was even rare to see a sports photograph printed in a newspaper. The only way to see sports played was by going to a game, and games were everywhere. Each town had at least one baseball team; the larger the community, the more plentiful the teams. Entire towns turned out to watch sandlot, high school, town, semipro, and minor league games.

Semipro teams often acted as a transition to the minor leagues. Young men playing for these teams could earn a small income while going to school or working. While still in high school, Dutch Stengel began to pitch for a semipro team, the Kansas City Red Sox. Dutch began earning $1.50 per game, but as his performance improved, he demanded a raise and won an increase to $3.00.

During the spring of 1908, the team traveled as far as Utah. The Red Sox provided Stengel with the opportunity to play high-quality baseball every day, and traveling with the team also gave him his first glimpse of the world outside

Kansas City. Going from city to city by train, the players were constantly together. On rainy days, they played basketball in local gymnasiums. During their off-hours, they engaged in pranks such as placing a snake in someone's bed or dousing an unsuspecting individual with a bucket of water. For a high school student, the travel and fun made up for the meager salary.

The following spring, the 18-year-old Stengel was back pitching for Central High. The pinnacle of his season came when he pitched a 7–6 thriller against Joplin High in the state tourna-

Stengel (fourth from right) during his early years in the minor leagues. When he first began to play for money, he was paid $1.50 per game.

ment. Central High's yearbook stated, "The baseball team this year was strong in every way, with the feature the hurling of Stengel." On the heels of that victory, Stengel resumed traveling with the Kansas City Red Sox.

Dutch completed four years at Central High in January 1910, but he lacked the credits necessary to graduate. When the Kansas City Blues offered him a contract, he decided to go for it. The Blues played in the American Association, the highest level of minor league ball, and were one step from the majors. However, Dutch needed his father's permission to join the team. One day, as Louis Stengel read the newspaper, Dutch abruptly stuck the papers under his father's nose. "Here, Pop, sign this will you?"

"What is it?" inquired the elder Stengel.

"It's a contract to play ball with the Blues. You have to sign it because I'm under 21."

"What about school?" his father asked.

"Ah, I'm finished with school," Dutch replied. "The Blues will pay me a salary of $135 a month."

In 1910, a monthly salary of $135 was too good to turn down. It far exceeded any income Dutch could earn elsewhere. "So, I put down my paper and signed," Louis Stengel recalled. "You never could change that boy's mind anyway."

3

"THE PET OF THE POPULACE"

Before Stengel went to the Blues training camp, he received a piece of advice from a neighbor, Charles "Kid" Nichols, a former National League pitcher. "I understand you get in a lot of trouble and arguments," said Nichols. "Don't be arguing all the time. Listen to your manager, or if you have an old player teaching you, listen to him. Never say, 'I won't do that.' Always listen. If you're not going to do what he says, don't tell him so. Let it go in one ear and let it roll around in there for a month, and then if it isn't any good, let it go out the other ear. But if it is good, memorize it and keep it. You do that and you'll keep out of a lot of trouble." Stengel never forgot Nichols's advice about listening to veteran players, but he had more difficulty curbing his appetite for arguments.

When Stengel joined the Blues at their camp in Excelsior Springs, Missouri, no one paid much attention to him. At the first exhibition game, the manager, Danny Shay, appointed Stengel water boy, and he had to carry the team's water buckets onto the field. Several of his high school friends were in the stands and yelled, "Water boy! Water boy!" When he pitched, Stengel's deliveries were pounded. Shay was not impressed by Stengel's pitching, but he did like

Stengel in 1911, when he was struggling to establish himself as a professional ballplayer. During the off-season, he began to attend dental school, where he kept the other students entertained with his elaborate pranks.

the way the rookie swung the bat. Determined to make him a hitter, Shay placed Stengel in the outfield, where he experienced new difficulties. When balls bounced off the wall, Shay would yell, "Play the angles! Play the angles!"

"If you want someone to play the angles," bellowed the brash young Stengel, "why don't you hire a pool player?"

"You ought to be a pool player," screamed Shay. "You've got a head as hard as a billiard ball." The nickname Billiard Ball stuck with Stengel for several days.

Despite the rookie's weaknesses, Shay saw that he could hit, throw, and run. He assigned Stengel to two veteran players, William "Spike" Shannon and Patsy Flaherty. Working with Stengel for hours, they taught him the finer points of outfielding, and to break up the monotonous hours of practice, they would allow him to hit occasionally.

Shay felt that Stengel still needed more instruction, so the rookie packed his cardboard suitcase and headed for Kankakee, Illinois, in the Class C Northern League. There he worked on fundamentals, especially sliding. In July, the Northern League collapsed, and Stengel was reassigned to Shelbyville, Kentucky, in the Class D Blue Grass League. In just a few brief months, he had gone from the top to the bottom of the minor league system. He stayed in Shelbyville only one month before the team was sold and moved to Maysville, Kentucky. In the few remaining weeks of the Blue Grass season, Stengel won a box of candy, a safety razor kit, and a hat—gifts from Maysville's merchants for his fireworks at the plate. For the last few games of the year, Stengel returned to the

Kansas City Blues and played before his hometown fans.

The following spring, Stengel reported to the Blues' Class C team in Aurora, Illinois. He batted .352 but almost got into serious trouble. During a game against Rockford, Stengel argued bitterly with the home plate umpire after being called out on strikes three times in a row. The third time, the umpire laughed and said, "You're out, big shot." Returning to the dugout, Stengel saw the ump crouching to call the next pitch. He picked up a bat, tiptoed to the plate, and whacked the unsuspecting ump across the behind. The crowd went crazy. Rockford was awarded the game on forfeit. Stengel drew a fine from the league office but somehow escaped suspension.

During the 1911 season, Larry Sutton, a Brooklyn Dodgers scout, was passing through Chicago. He had heard about Stengel's hot bat and caught a train to Aurora just in time to see Stengel perform at the plate. Sutton listed the young outfielder as a good prospect, and the Dodgers drafted him in August.

During spring training in 1912, a veteran player, Norman "Tabasco Kid" Elberfeld, took a liking to the 21-year-old Stengel and taught him the finer points of the game, including the technique of getting hit by a pitch when the team needed a baserunner. At the end of spring training, the Dodgers sent Stengel to Montgomery, Alabama, in the Class AA Southern Association. Stengel batted only .250 but led all Southern Association outfielders in assists. The Dodgers announced that he would join them in Brooklyn when the Southern Association's season ended in September.

Stengel poses for photographers in 1913, his first full major league season. The 23-year-old rookie batted .272 for the year and impressed the fans with his play in center field.

Stengel arrived in New York on a Monday afternoon, September 16, after a long overnight train ride from Montgomery. He went directly to the Dodgers' home field, Washington Park. In those days, games began at 3:30, and Casey watched the "big fellows," as he called them, lose to Pittsburgh, their 86th defeat of the season. He was sure that he could not do any worse than his new teammates were doing.

The following day, Stengel put on a major league uniform for the first time. When manager Bill Dahlen told Stengel he would be playing center field and batting second, the rookie was surprised and elated. In his first at-bat, he slapped a single to center. The next time up, he singled again, driving in a runner from second. The score was tied 3–3 when Stengel batted again in the fourth. He slammed his third straight hit to drive in another run and put the team in the lead. He then stole second. "The crowd was busy applauding the young man all afternoon," wrote a newspaper reporter. He got another hit, stole second again, and, facing the fourth pitcher of the afternoon, walked and stole second once more. Another sportswriter dubbed him "The pet of the populace . . . the fair-haired youth."

Ebbets Field, Brooklyn's new ballpark, opened before 25,000 fans on a cold, windy Saturday, April 9, 1913. When Stengel hit the first regular-season home run at Ebbets Field to beat the Giants, a sportswriter wrote, "Charley Stengel, who whizzed dizzily across the Superba horizon in 1912 [sportswriters also referred to the Dodgers as the Superbas and Robbie's Robins], added to his laurels yesterday." Praising Stengel's glove work in center field, the writer

Brooklyn players witness Ebbets Field's first flag-raising ceremony on April 9, 1913. Stengel hit the first home run at the new ballpark, which remained the home of the Dodgers until they moved to Los Angeles in 1958.

also declared, "He ate up five flies in a half gale." But Stengel sprained his ankle on July 4 and played poorly for the remainder of the season.

Toward the end of the season, an actor named DeWitt Hopper began reciting Ernest Thayer's classic baseball poem, "Casey at the Bat," on the vaudeville circuit. After that, whenever the slumping Stengel struck out with men on base, the crowd would yell, "Hey, there's Casey at the bat again." By 1914, the fans and the press were using the nickname regularly, and it stuck to Stengel for the rest of his life.

4

"STENGEL IS SPECTACULAR"

A new major league, the Federal League, opened for business in 1914. Attempting to lure good players from the two existing leagues, the Feds offered big salaries, forcing the National and American League owners to give their players raises. Stengel had earned $2,100 in 1913; the Dodgers boosted him to $4,000 to keep him from switching leagues.

In January, Stengel had his first stab at instructing other players when he helped coach at the University of Mississippi before joining the Dodgers in Augusta, Georgia. Stengel was full of stories about his adventures on the Mississippi campus, and he soon had another nickname—Professor. He found that he truly liked the teaching aspect of baseball; as he gained confidence, he frequently began to share his ideas with teammates.

Stengel was not the only one with ideas. During spring training, Brooklyn manager Wilbert "Robbie" Robinson told Stengel to play right field. Stengel resisted the move. Robinson explained that a left-handed thrower in right field would have an easier time throwing after fielding base hits along the foul line. To prove his point, Robinson took Stengel, his new center fielder, Joe Riggert, and a group of sportswriters to right

Stengel demonstrates his batting style in a photograph taken in 1914. During the season, Stengel learned a new position, right field, and raised his batting average to .316.

field one day and had balls hit to the two outfielders. The writers agreed that Stengel got his throws off more quickly than the right-handed Riggert. Years later, Robinson said, "I made a real good right fielder out of Stengel, and against his wishes."

During the winter of 1915, Stengel suffered a severe case of typhoid fever and was hospitalized. When he reported to spring training in March, he was pale and thin. His face was drawn, and he weighed only 157 pounds, 20 pounds under his playing weight. Although his batting average sank to .150, Stengel's fielding dramatically improved. His hours of practice in learning to "play the angles" of the right-field wall at Ebbets Field began to pay off, and he also became adept at catching balls hit into the sun.

Stengel and the Dodgers went all the way to win the pennant in 1916. Brooklyn's catcher,

Brooklyn's top four outfielders in 1916 were (left to right) Stengel, Jimmy Johnston, Hi Meyers, and Zack Wheat. Wheat, a future Hall of Famer, played nearly every day, while Stengel, Johnston, and Myers were platooned by Manager Wilbert Robinson.

Chief Myers, later told Larry Ritter in *The Glory of Their Times*, "I always maintain that Stengel won one more pennant than the records show. That was in 1916 with Brooklyn. It was Casey who kept us on our toes. He was the life of the party and kept us old-timers pepped up all season." The Dodgers lost the World Series to the Red Sox in five games, but Stengel's batting average for the Series was .364, the highest on the team.

When the Federal League folded in 1915, players' salaries in both the American and National Leagues dropped drastically. Stengel's earnings had been up to $6,000, but in 1916, Charles Ebbets cut him down to $4,600. The New York sportswriters rallied around Stengel. "Because of his clowning Stengel is lightly esteemed as a player by many folks who should know better," wrote one. "The truth is that it's doubtful whether there is a man on the Brooklyn ball team who has more baseball instinct than this comical cuss." Another writer declared, "Stengel is spectacular, even when doing nothing in particular."

The United States entered World War I on April 6, 1917, as another baseball season began. Angered by his salary cut, Stengel was openly critical of Ebbets to the press, and this did not sit well with the owner. The Dodgers dropped to seventh place, and after the season, Ebbets traded Stengel to Pittsburgh. In his sixth year of baseball, Stengel found himself earning the same $2,100 that he had received in his second year of play. "With the salary I get," said Stengel, "I'm so hollow and starving that if I slide I'm liable to explode like a light bulb."

One day, during a game against the Giants in the Polo Grounds, the frustrations of the past two years erupted in Stengel. When umpire Pete Harrison called him out on a slide into second, Stengel flew into a rage and was thrown out of the game. Ripping his shirt off, he handed it to Harrison. "Here, why don't you play on our side for a change?" Stengel bellowed. The next day, Stengel received a telegram from league president John Tener, informing him that he had been fined $25 for his poor conduct. Stengel played the next game with the yellow telegram pinned on his uniform sleeve.

Three days later, Stengel enlisted in the navy; but the war ended in November, and he was back in baseball for the 1919 season. When he was traded to the last-place Phillies on August 9, an angry Stengel went home and did not report to the Phillies until the spring of 1920. Despite his unhappiness, he batted .292 for the Phillies, his highest average to date. In 1921, a series of injuries kept him out of the lineup for much of the season. But he began to feel much better when he learned that he had been traded to the New York Giants, one of baseball's premier teams.

John McGraw, the hard-nosed 5-foot-7-inch Giants manager, was fittingly known as Mugsy and Little Napoleon. "I learned more from John McGraw than anybody," Stengel later said. McGraw, who finished his 33-year managerial career with 2,840 victories and 10 pennants to his credit, became Stengel's hero. Stengel respected McGraw's knowledge of the game and his no-nonsense approach. "He wanted you to be a fighter at the plate, stand in there, don't back off. Get a piece of the ball, something might

Stengel and his New York Giants teammates work out with a medicine ball during spring training at San Antonio, Texas, in 1923. Though 32 years old, Stengel was coming off his finest major league season, during which he had batted .368.

happen," remembered Stengel. "He'd get very disturbed if you didn't get up there and fight the pitcher."

Despite Stengel's injuries, McGraw admired his spirited approach to baseball: "Stengel is an old man in a baseball sense [he was 31], but he is the most vigorous old man I ever saw." Although his physical ailments limited his participation that year, Stengel enjoyed sitting on the bench as the Giants won the 1921 World Series. "I made more money sitting with the Giants than I ever made standing with anyone else," he reflected.

Stengel's physical condition improved, and he hit .368 in the 1922 season as the Giants repeated as world champions. In 1923, Stengel had another solid year, finishing at .339. That fall, the newly built Yankee Stadium hosted its first World Series, and 55,307 fans filled the big ballpark to see the Giants face the Yankees in the opener. The game was tied 4–4 in the top of the ninth when Stengel stepped up to the plate. Yankees pitcher Joe Bush recalled, "The count was 3–2 and I threw just as hard as I could. He crashed it good and plenty." Stengel's hard liner to left-center field found the gap in Yankee

Stengel slides across home plate for an inside-the-park home run after driving a ball into the left-center-field gap in Yankee Stadium. His run gave the Giants a 5–4 win over the Yankees in the opening game of the 1923 World Series.

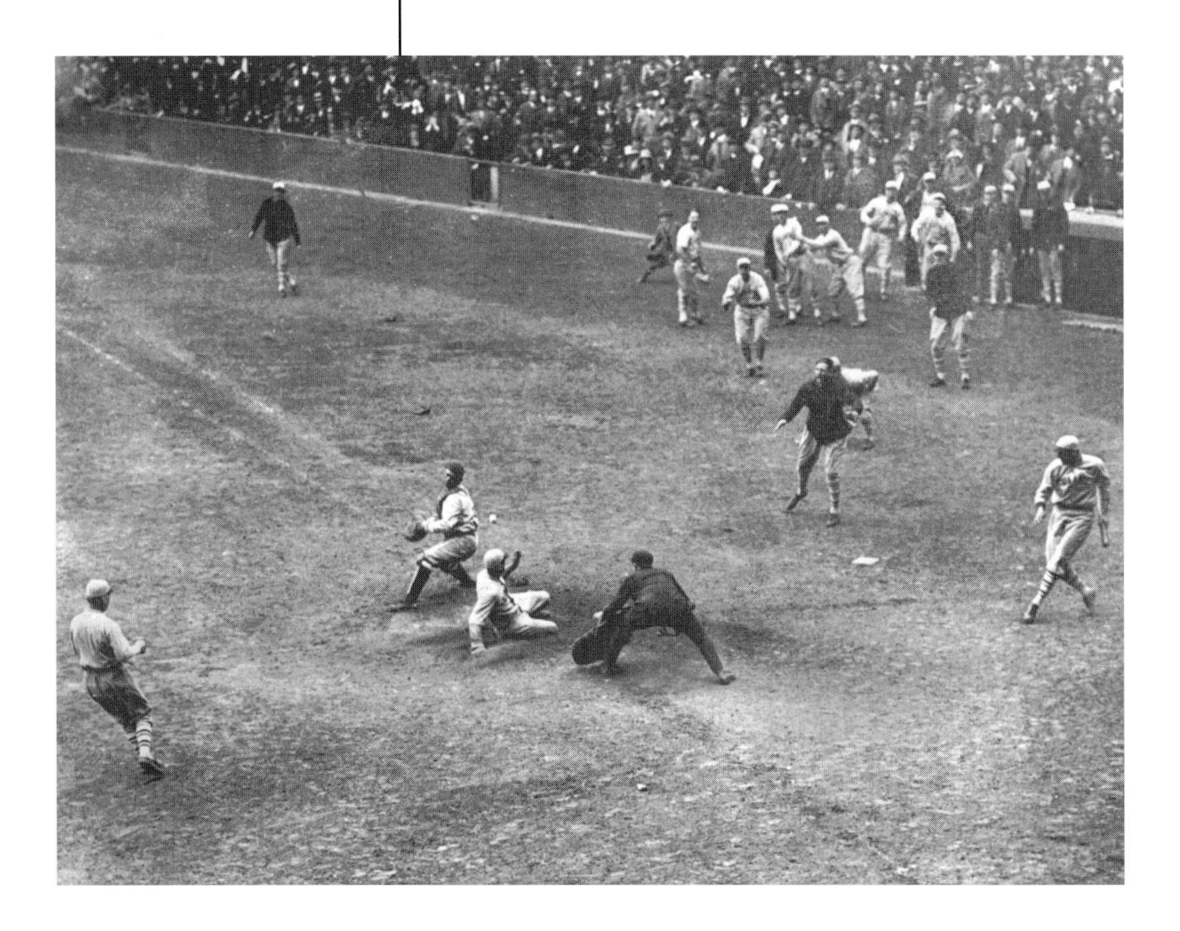

Stadium's famed "Death Valley." Sportswriter Heywood Broun wrote, "The outfielders turned and ran toward the bleacher wall, and the ball sailed and hopped and skipped, and Stengel sprinted. The Giants won 5–4—Stengel slid into home, came up on one knee, and waved to the crowd." The New York *American*'s account of the game ran under the following subhead: "60,000 Frantic Fans Screech as Casey Beats Ball to Plate—Warped Legs, Twisted, Bent in Years of Campaigning, Last Until He Reaches Goal."

In the third game, Yankees hurler Sad Sam Jones had a shutout entering the seventh inning when Stengel stepped up to the plate. He hammered Jones's pitch into the bleachers for another game-winning homer. As Stengel rounded the bases, he looked at Jones, thumbed his nose, and threw a kiss at the Yankees dugout.

Following the game, Stengel was interviewed by a female reporter, Zoe Buckley. When she asked Stengel why players did not like interviews, he responded, "We know the hazards—we're the hero today and the goat tomorrow. It only goes to show you that good luck is as sure to stumble your way as bad luck. You've got to learn how to take both. You have to remember that nothing lasts—neither the good nor the bad." Stengel held to this philosophy all his life. The proof of it came when the Yankees, who had lost the two previous World Series to the Giants, rallied to win this one, 4 games to 2.

5

CASEY AT THE HELM

Soon after the Giants lost the 1923 World Series to the Yankees, Casey Stengel had more proof that good things do not last. The practical McGraw traded his "old man" to the lowly Boston Braves. Stengel observed, "The paths of glory lead but to the Braves."

In August 1924, Stengel married his fiancée, Edna Lawson, while the Braves were playing in St. Louis. In the off-season, the couple made their home in Glendale, California. The next year, 35-year-old Stengel's major league career ended. The Braves sent him to their Worcester, Massachusetts, team, making him the club's president as well as the player-manager.

Under Stengel's guidance, the Worcester team climbed from the cellar to finish a respectable third. The Toledo, Ohio, team of the American Association wanted to hire him as their manager for 1926, and Stengel wanted to make the move. Using his authority as Worcester's president, Stengel fired himself as manager. Then he resigned as president and packed his bags for Toledo. He managed the Toledo club, known as the Mud Hens, through six eventful seasons.

Stengel's ideas for motivating his players were often unusual. Following the crash of the stock market in 1929, the country fell into the Great

Stengel stands behind six of his Toledo Mud Hens at the opening of the 1926 American Association season. On several occasions during his six seasons at Toledo, Stengel was threatened with arrest after he incited the hometown fans to attack the umpires.

Depression, and everyone was worried about the economy. "Now, you boys haven't been playing very well," he told the team one day, "but I know there's been a lot on your minds. I see a lot of you reading about the stock market, and I know you're thinking about it. Now, I'm gonna give you a tip on the market. Buy Pennsylvania Railroad because if you don't start playing better ball there's gonna be so many of you riding trains outta here that railroad stocks are a cinch to go up!"

The nation's economy continued to worsen, affecting every aspect of life, including baseball.

Edna Lawson Stengel, photographed in 1925 as she put the finishing touches on a pie. One of Casey's Toledo players recalled that the manager had "a lot of love and admiration for his wife . . . and he would try to work her into a story if he was trying to teach a young player something."

The Mud Hens suffered financially, and the team folded following the 1931 season. The 41-year-old Stengel was out of a job for the first time since he had signed with Kansas City in 1910—but not for long.

In December 1931, the Dodgers hired Stengel as a coach. With the depression raging, there was no money to buy players, and the Dodgers' fortunes waned for several years. When Stengel became the team's manager in 1934, he realized he lacked quality players but saw the opportunity to bring some young players along. "What else are you going to do when you get a second-division ball club?" he said. "You got a couple of young players on it, you work on them. . . . You keep after them. You ask them why they didn't make that throw. You ask them why they played that man there. Then for somebody else they turn out to be good ballplayers, but what of it? You helped to make them good ballplayers, didn't you?"

Stengel tempered his frustrations with a sense of humor. He found his outrageous infielder-outfielder, Frenchy Bordagaray, to be especially amusing. One day, the umpire called Frenchy out on a pickoff play at second base, even though it appeared that he was standing right on the bag. Stengel shot out of the dugout and started yelling at the umpire. To his amazement, Frenchy said, "No, he's right, Case. I'm out."

"How could you be out?" Stengel shouted. "You were standing on second base."

"I was tapping my foot," Frenchy explained, "and I guess he got me between taps."

On another occasion, Stengel was coaching third when Frenchy got to second base. Stengel

Stengel looks troubled as he watches his Boston Bees in spring training in March 1938. However, the Bees played respectably during the season, finishing 2 games above .500.

gave Bordagaray the sign to remain on second, but Frenchy ignored the sign and stole third. After Bordagaray slid in safely, Stengel said, "I ought to fine you for that."

"With the lead I had," Frenchy quipped, "you ought to fine yourself for not inviting me over."

The Dodgers never rose above fifth place, and at the end of the 1936 season, the 47-year-old Stengel was, as he liked to put it, "discharged" once again. The Dodgers had signed Stengel to a two-year contract, so they actually paid him not to manage the second season. He stayed out of baseball entirely during 1937. Instead, he and Edna went to Texas; they had made some investments in Texas oil, and they wanted to learn more about the business.

In 1938, the Stengels made a new investment. The Boston Braves had new owners and (temporarily) a new name, the Bees. The Stengels put $43,000 into the club, and Casey became the manager. With Stengel at the helm for four years, the Bees never finished higher than sixth place in the National League. While he tried to teach the game to his "ribbon clerks" (his term for poor ballplayers), defeat was difficult for Stengel. Following the loss of a double-header one day, he sagged into a barber's chair and requested a shave. "But don't bother to cut my throat," he instructed, "I might want to do that myself later on."

NY
NY

6

"FUNNY LIKE A FOX"

On December 7, 1941, the United States entered World War II following the Japanese attack on Pearl Harbor. Many baseball players and administrators went away to war, including Bill Veeck, owner of the Milwaukee Brewers of the American Association. In his absence, the Brewers hired Casey Stengel to manage the team in 1944. When Veeck learned that Stengel had been hired as his team's manager, he was livid. He wrote an angry letter to his subordinates, calling Stengel a second-division manager who did not care if his teams won. Ironically, Stengel won a pennant for the first time in his career. Responding to praise for his managerial performance, he simply said, "I had the horses."

When Veeck returned from the war and learned of his team's success under Stengel, he deeply regretted sending the letter. He begged Stengel to stay on as manager, but Stengel would have none of it. Instead, he accepted a position in 1945 to manage the Yankees' American Association farm team in Kansas City. The war ended that summer; once more, ballparks were filled, and the sport welcomed home many players who had served their country. After the season, however, the Yankees had new owners, and

Stengel and his injured superstar, Joe DiMaggio, confer at the bat rack before a 1949 game at Yankee Stadium. Though the two men managed to get along in public, they heartily disliked one another.

Stengel was unemployed once more. He returned to his home in California and signed on to manage the Oakland Oaks of the Pacific Coast League.

Stengel managed the Oaks from 1946 through 1948. Recalling Stengel as a manager, one of the veteran Oaks said, "If we won a double-header Casey would come into the clubhouse and say, 'You fellas did pretty well today and it's up to me to buy you each a three-dollar dinner.' " Three dollars bought a good meal in those days. The player recalled that when the Oaks beat the Los Angeles Angels in a double-header in the 1946 playoffs, "Casey came in and said, 'Every man here rates a ten-dollar dinner from the old man.' Next day he passed out ten bucks apiece to twenty-seven men—from his own pocket. No wonder we played our butts off for him."

In 1949, the 59-year-old Stengel got the biggest challenge of his life. He was asked to manage the mighty New York Yankees, who had won eight pennants in 13 years while Stengel had bounced from the minors to the majors and back again several times. During his first press conference as the Yankees manager, the usually jolly Stengel was uncharacteristically nervous. "I've been hired to win, and I think I will," he said. "There is less wrong with the Yankees than any club I've had."

Stengel and his biggest star, Joe DiMaggio, could not have been more opposite in their personalities or in their approach to baseball. DiMaggio immediately disliked Stengel and, to make matters worse, told a reporter that Stengel did not know what he was doing when he shuffled players in and out of the lineup and changed their positions from day to day. He told teammate Phil Rizzuto, "I don't get this guy. Nobody knows when he's playing or where. With this guy managing, we can't possibly win."

Stengel knew how Dimaggio felt about him. Furthermore, he knew that some of the other players, including Rizzuto, shared DiMaggio's feelings. Stengel said, "The secret to managing is to keep the players who hate you away from the players who are undecided." However, some of the newer players liked Stengel. Infielder Jerry Coleman, outfielder Gene Woodling, and a young catcher named Yogi Berra all felt that they had things to learn from Stengel. Woodling later said, "Casey was a heck of a psychiatrist. Don't kid yourself. That guy made me successful. I was mad at him a lot of times, and said things about him, but he got good baseball out of me. . . . He knew who to stir up and who to leave alone."

When the Yankees were hit by injuries, Stengel resorted to platooning his players: he moved outfielders Hank Bauer, Johnny Lindell, Gene Woodling, and Cliff Mapes in and out of the lineup, according to his needs. The players disliked the strategy because it meant that most of them played fewer games. Woodling remembered, "Bauer and I used to tell him we wanted to play. And when we didn't play it made us mad and we told him off. Bauer and I could have killed the old man lots of times." But Stengel realized their anger would turn to action on the field. He said, "Those square heads, when I turn 'em loose, they're going to go out and beat somebody."

When the Yankees went on to capture the pennant and the World Series, the Yankees organization was hailed as brilliant for hiring the Old

Professor. "I knew what I was getting," said Yankees general manager George Weiss, one of baseball's shrewdest executives. "I was not hiring a comedian. What did they think, that he learned how to manage all at once in 1949?" Years later, Detroit Tigers manager Sparky Anderson admiringly summed up Stengel's deceptive wisdom: "Casey was funny like a fox."

After just one World Series win with the New York Yankees, everyone looked to Stengel as baseball's newest mastermind. Writers dissected his "new" style of managing. They praised his uncanny ability to know just when to take a pitcher out of the game and his practice of warming up two relievers at a time. He was later credited with inventing the modern pitching staff, which included a "closer" whose specialty was pitching the last inning when his team held the lead.

Platooning, which had been around since the days of McGraw, was suddenly "discovered" as a Stengel idea. Speaking with his characteristic flair for the English language, Stengel recalled, "Late in the season everyone was talking about

Stengel positions his infielders during Game 3 of the 1949 World Series. After he guided the Yankees to the world championship in his first year as manager, Stengel finally received credit for the wealth of baseball knowledge he possessed.

platooning the players, which I very much did, but we come to a point against Boston where it comes down to this. I had to win two games to win the pennant. I was gonna platoon myself out of a job, or platoon myself in, which is what happened as I am certain you recall."

Although Stengel realized that he had indeed "platooned himself into a job" as the Yankees skipper, he was not able to rest on the laurels of one World Series win. At the beginning of spring training in 1950, Stengel told the players, "Last year is history. Forget it. There's no point in looking back. We gotta go out and beat 'em all over again this year." His management style had been unusually subdued during his first year in New York. The Yankees were about to see the real Stengel.

Phil Rizzuto felt that winning the pennant changed Stengel. The shortstop reported that Stengel became loud and sarcastic. "We'd have clubhouse meetings that would last an hour . . . and he'd talk the whole time," Rizzuto recalled. The confidence Stengel felt after winning the World Series also changed his kid-glove treatment of DiMaggio. While he publicly praised the great slugger, saying he was the best player he had ever managed, he no longer feared DiMaggio's ego. When DiMaggio went into a hitting slump, Stengel benched him for a few days without bothering to notify him. When the press questioned his decision, Stengel responded, "So what if he doesn't talk to me? I'll get by, and so will he. DiMaggio doesn't get paid to talk to me and I don't either. He's getting paid to play ball and I'm getting paid to manage. If what I'm doing is wrong, my bosses will fire me. I've been fired lots of places before."

Though the Yankees veterans continued to resent Stengel, they could not deny his success as their skipper. In September, the Yankees overtook the Tigers to win the pennant by three games. They went on to sweep the Phillies in the 1950 World Series.

Following the Series, Gene Woodling went into Stengel's office. He wanted to apologize to "the old man" for some of the things he had done during the season, but he never got the chance. "Get out of here," said Stengel. "You ain't coming in here telling me you're sorry for making me look good all season."

In 1951, Stengel introduced instructional schools for young players prior to the regular spring-training camp. Reporting to that first instructional school in 1951 was a 19-year-old out of the Oklahoma Ozarks, Mickey Mantle. A shortstop who had spent two years in the minors, Mantle displayed rare skill and power. Although everyone saw Mantle's potential, George Weiss wanted Mantle to spend more time in the minors. Stengel disagreed. DiMaggio had retired, and the manager felt that his other outfielders were fading. He convinced Weiss to keep Mantle on the big club and switch him to center field. Although Mantle struggled at first to master his new position, his bat was crucial to the Yankees' success that season. After overtaking the Indians in September, the Yankees went on to defeat the Giants in the World Series. In his three seasons with the Yankees, Stengel had won three world championships.

When the Yankees defeated the Dodgers in the 1952 World Series, Stengel matched the accomplishments of John McGraw and of his greatest predecessor at the Yankees helm, Joe

Stengel gives advice to rookie Mickey Mantle in August 1951. At first, the 20-year-old slugger could hardly believe that his gray-haired manager had once been a ballplayer. "He thinks I was born 60 years old," Stengel said.

McCarthy—both men had won four straight pennants, and McCarthy's teams had also won the World Series each time (McGraw's went 2-2). If Stengel could win again in 1953, he would pass both men in the record books.

When the 1953 Yankees won 18 straight games in June, they tore the pennant race open. Filled with zeal throughout the streak, Stengel shouted at his club, "Don't let 'em up. Don't let 'em up." And there was no letting up until the Yankees defeated the Dodgers yet again for their fifth straight World Series triumph. "You know," said Stengel, "John McGraw was a great man in New York and he won pennants. But Stengel is in town now, and he's won a lot of pennants too."

Stengel had to settle for five in a row. In 1954, the Indians had a brilliant campaign, winning a record 111 games, and took the pennant home to Cleveland. It was hard for Stengel to admit that his mighty empire might crumble. He blamed much of the Yankees' change of fortune on the failure of Mickey Mantle to develop into the kind of player that Stengel had envisioned. Though hitting close to .300, Mantle had not yet cracked the 30-home-run barrier, and chronic leg injuries often kept him out of the lineup.

The Yankees bounced back to win pennants in 1955, 1956, 1957, and 1958 and won the World Series in 1956 and 1958. As they dominated baseball year after year, the legend of their colorful manager grew. The country became familiar with Stengel's peculiar jargon and his rambling interviews. One time, a reporter asked him a question, and Stengel talked for 40 minutes. "Casey," the reporter finally interrupted, "You haven't answered my question." Not missing a beat, Stengel replied, "Don't rush me."

It seemed as though Stengel did not want to be rushed through any part of his experience as the Yankees manager. He had won 9 flags in 10 years, and he was savoring every moment of the long, golden decade.

In 1959, the Yankees had an off year, and the Chicago White Sox, led by Minnie Minoso and

Catcher Yogi Berra leaps into the arms of Don Larsen after the final out of Game 5 of the 1956 World Series. Larsen had just beaten the Dodgers, 2–0, pitching the only perfect game in World Series history.

Nellie Fox, took the pennant. However, during the off-season, George Weiss acquired Roger Maris in a trade with the Kansas City Athletics. The left-handed-hitting slugger flourished in Yankee Stadium, with its short right field, and emerged as a superstar, clouting 39 home runs and winning the Most Valuable Player Award. (The following year, he would hit 61 balls out of the park, eclipsing Babe Ruth's seemingly unbreakable record.) The Yankees held off the threatening Orioles, winning 15 consecutive games in September, to clinch Stengel's 10th pennant. When the Yankees lost the World Series to Pittsburgh on Bill Mazeroski's home run in the final game, it was a bitter blow to a team that expected to win every year.

Five days after the World Series, the Yankees called a press conference. To the astonishment of many fans, team officials read a statement announcing that Stengel was retiring at the age of 70. When questioned by reporters, Stengel said, "I'm just sorry Casey isn't fifty years old, but all business comes down to the point where it's best for the future to make a change." He added, "I'll never make the mistake of being seventy again." No one doubted that he was being forced out, and many of the same experts who had ridiculed his hiring in 1949 now wondered how the Yankees could dispense with a man who had won 10 pennants and 7 World Series in 11 years.

The next evening, the Yankees threw a banquet in Stengel's honor at New York's Waldorf-Astoria Hotel. "Don't give up," Stengel told the assembled crowd. "Tomorrow is just another day, and that's myself."

7

THE AMAZIN' METS

On October 2, 1961, the new National League team, the New York Mets, held a press conference to announce the name of their first manager—Charles Dillon Stengel. Ironically, the conference was held in the same room in which the Yankees had announced Stengel's "retirement" a year earlier.

In 1962, Stengel arrived in St. Petersburg, Florida, for the first Mets spring training camp, bringing with him a suitcase and 50 seasons of baseball experience. But Stengel saw unsettling changes in the players: "You tell them, 'Here is an opportunity,' and the youth of America says, 'Where is the money?' "

Dealing with "ribbon clerks" and over-the-hill veterans was not a new experience for Stengel. However, when the Mets faced the Yankees in an exhibition game, Stengel played to win. When the Mets defeated the Yankees 4–3, New Yorkers paid attention. Stengel loved the coverage in the press, but he was not expecting too much from his team. "I ain't fooled," he said, "They play different when the other side is trying too." Although the Mets won almost as many games as they lost in spring training, Stengel realized he had little talent to work with and that the season would be rough. All the same,

On October 18, 1960, Stengel explains to the press that he is being forced to retire as Yankees manager because of his age. "I'll never make the mistake of being seventy again," Stengel quipped.

Stengel beamed as New Yorkers welcomed their new team with a huge parade up Broadway. A writer who covered the event had the following description of the craggy-featured, white-haired manager: "Stengel had the look of an eagle that had just flown through an ice storm."

Stengel's predictions proved accurate. The Mets played miserably. They elevated incompetence to new heights and caused Stengel to lament, "Can't anybody play this here game?" His question became the unofficial Mets motto. By mid-May, they were in last place for good, on their way to a record 120 losses. The long road trips were tiring for the aging manager. After one all-night flight, the Mets reached their hotel in Houston at 8:00 A.M. As the press waited for Stengel outside his room, the manager quipped to an assistant, "Tell them I'm being embalmed."

A love affair quickly developed between New Yorkers and their terrible new team. Sensing that the Mets were trying their best despite their incredible lack of talent, fans embraced the losing club and cheered them wildly on the rare occasions when they turned a play well. Bitter over the loss of their beloved Giants and Dodgers, who had moved to California in 1958, they took the beleaguered Mets and Stengel to their hearts. The sight of the elderly manager sprinting out to the mound to remove another hapless pitcher was enough to drive the home crowd into a frenzy.

Mets fans especially adored their first baseman, Marvelous Marv Throneberry, who was equally inept as a fielder, hitter, and baserunner. Typical of his performance, he once managed to hit a triple but was called out for not touching first base. When Stengel heard the

Stengel, General Manager George Weiss, and other members of the New York Mets gather on the steps of New York's City Hall at the beginning of the 1962 baseball season. The 1962 Mets lost more games than any team in major league history, but baseball-hungry New Yorkers loved them all the same.

call, he exploded out of the dugout and confronted the first-base umpire. While he was arguing, the second-base umpire strolled over and reported, "I hate to tell you this, Casey, but he missed second base, too." Glaring at both umpires, Stengel barked, "Well, I know he touched third base because he's standing on it."

As Stengel watched the team's poor play from the dugout, he never ceased to be amazed by his club's creativity in fouling up the most routine situations. "I've been in this game a hundred years," observed Stengel, "but I see new ways to lose that I never knew existed before." One day in St. Louis, Stengel got into a taxi outside the ballpark with a group of sportswriters. The driver asked the writers, "Are you guys baseball players?" "No," snapped Stengel, "and neither are my players players."

The Mets moved into their new home, Shea Stadium, in 1964, but their fortunes did not improve. Although the Mets drew good crowds, the fans were tiring of their club's permanent residence in the cellar. The front office secretly hoped that Stengel might throw in the towel. He was almost 75 years old, and some felt the club needed a younger manager. However, when the 1965 spring training camp opened, Stengel was there, as feisty as ever.

The Mets planned pregame ceremonies to help Stengel celebrate his 75th birthday on July 30. On the evening of July 25, a dinner was held at Toots Shor's restaurant for the old-timers arriving to help Stengel celebrate. However, Stengel fell at the restaurant and broke his hip. He never managed again. On August 30, he announced his retirement. "If I can't run out there and take a pitcher out," Stengel told reporters, "I'm not capable of continuing managing."

On September 2, the Mets honored Stengel during an unusual ceremony held several hours prior to the game in an empty stadium. As his number 37 was retired, Stengel said, "I'd like to see them give that number to some young player so it can go on and do some good for the Mets."

Casey and Edna retired to their home in Glendale, California, but Casey remained a visible figure at many baseball functions. Walking with a cane while his hip mended, Stengel showed up at the Mets 1966 spring training camp in St. Petersburg, Florida, remarking, "I don't really need this [the cane], but I have to limp or I can't get into the Hall of Fame."

Stengel assumed he would have to wait the required five years before being eligible for the Hall of Fame. However, in a rare action, officials held a secret meeting in which they waived the rule and voted to induct Stengel immediately. On March 8, while Stengel was still in St. Petersburg, the Mets called a press conference. They surprised both Stengel and the public with the announcement of his induction. Stengel observed,"It's a terrific thing to get it while you're still alive." After that day, Stengel always added "Hall of Fame" to his signature.

Stengel was officially inducted into the Hall of Fame at Cooperstown, along with the great Boston Red Sox slugger Ted Williams, in the summer of 1966. During his acceptance speech, Stengel said, "I want to thank everybody. I want to thank some of the owners who were amazing to me, and those big presidents of the leagues who were so kind to me when I was obnoxious." He thanked his parents and his friend George

Edna and Casey Stengel, photographed during Casey's induction into the Hall of Fame on July 25, 1966. At the time, only four managers in major league history—Connie Mack, John McGraw, Bucky Harris, and Joe McCarthy—had more victories to their credit than did Stengel.

Weiss, "who would find out whenever I was discharged and would reemploy me."

Stengel attended every Hall of Fame induction until 1975. Feeling unwell that summer, he was hospitalized in Glendale. Rumors circulated that he had died. When a friend called to confirm this, Stengel picked up the phone and said, "I didn't die. I just lost my voice." In fact, Stengel had been diagnosed with lymphatic cancer. He was able to return home for a brief time, but he was hospitalized again in September and could do little but lie in bed watching baseball on television. When Tim McNamara, one of

Stengel's players 40 years earlier at Toledo, visited his former manager in the hospital, he found Stengel near death. "Although he was so weak," McNamara recalled, "he stuck his hand out from beneath the sheet to shake mine and whispered, 'Thank you for coming.' " Casey Stengel died on September 29, 1975, one day after the baseball season ended.

Stengel's funeral was postponed a full week so the services could be held on an off-day during the playoffs, allowing the maximum number of baseball people to attend. The funeral was really a happy occasion, as those in attendance recalled Stengel's wit and his love of the game.

Stengel's life was truly one to be celebrated. He had discovered baseball in his youth and had dedicated his life to the game. It brought him much joy, and he influenced the game as few individuals ever will. Once, when Stengel was asked about the secret of life, the Old Professor quipped, "The trick is growing up without growing old." Casey Stengel remained forever young in baseball.

OFFICIAL TIME

CHRONOLOGY

1890	Born Charles Dillon Stengel in Kansas City, Missouri, on July 30
1910	Signs with the Kansas City Blues of the American Association
1911	Drafted by the Brooklyn Dodgers
1912	Reports to the Dodgers Class AA Southern Association team in Montgomery, Alabama; plays in his first major league game with the Dodgers in Brooklyn on August 12
1918	Traded to the Pittsburgh Pirates after six seasons with the Dodgers
1922	Enjoys best season in the major leagues, batting .369 for the New York Giants
1923	Stars in the World Series as the Giants defeat the Yankees
1924	Marries Edna Lawson
1924–25	Finishes playing career with the Boston Braves
1925	Becomes a player-manager with Worcester
1926–30	Manages the Toledo Mud Hens of the American Association
1934–36	Manages the Brooklyn Dodgers
1938–43	Manages the Boston Bees in the National League
1944	Manages the Milwaukee Brewers of the American Association and wins pennant
1945	Manages the New York Yankees farm team in Kansas City
1946–48	Manages the Oakland Oaks of the Pacific Coast League
1949	Named manager of the New York Yankees; Yankees win pennant and World Series with Stengel at the helm
1953	Stengel becomes the first manager to win five consecutive World Series
1960	Retires as Yankees manager after winning 10th pennant in 12 years
1962	Becomes the first manager of the New York Mets
1965	Steps down as Mets manager after suffering broken hip; Mets retire Stengel's number 37
1966	Stengel is inducted into the Baseball Hall of Fame at Cooperstown, N.Y.
1975	Dies in Glendale, California, on September 29

CHARLES DILLON STENGEL
"CASEY"
MANAGED NEW YORK YANKEES 1949-1960.
WON 10 PENNANTS AND 7 WORLD SERIES WITH
NEW YORK YANKEES, ONLY MANAGER TO WIN
5 CONSECUTIVE WORLD SERIES 1949-1953.
PLAYED OUTFIELD 1912-1925 WITH BROOKLYN,
PITTSBURGH, PHILADELPHIA, NEW YORK AND
BOSTON N.L. TEAMS. MANAGED BROOKLYN
1934-1936, BOSTON BRAVES 1938-1943,
NEW YORK METS 1962-1965.

MAJOR LEAGUE STATISTICS

BOSTON BRAVES, BROOKLYN DODGERS, NEW YORK GIANTS, PHILADELPHIA PHILLIES, PITTSBURGH PIRATES

YEAR	TEAM	G	AB	R	H	2B	3B	HR	RBI	BA	SB
1912	BKN N	17	57	9	18	1	0	1	13	.316	5
1913		124	438	60	119	16	8	7	43	.272	19
1914		126	412	55	130	13	10	4	60	.316	19
1915		132	459	52	109	20	12	3	50	.237	5
1916		127	462	66	129	27	8	8	53	.279	11
1917		150	549	69	141	23	12	6	73	.257	18
1918	PIT N	39	122	18	30	4	1	1	12	.246	11
1919		89	321	38	94	10	10	4	43	.293	12
1920	PHI N	129	445	53	130	25	6	9	50	.292	7
1921	2 teams	PHI N (24G- .305) NY N (18G- .227)									
	total	42	81	11	23	4	1	0	6	.284	1
1922	NY N	84	250	48	92	8	10	7	48	.368	4
1923		75	218	39	74	11	5	5	43	.339	6
1924	BOS N	131	461	57	129	20	6	5	39	.280	13
1925		12	13	0	1	0	0	0	2	.077	0
Totals		1277	4288	575	1219	182	89	60	535	.284	131

FURTHER READING

Allen, Maury. *Now Wait a Minute, Casey!* New York: Doubleday, 1965.

———. *You Could Look It Up: The Life of Casey Stengel.* New York: Times Books, 1979.

Creamer, Robert W. *Stengel: His Life and Times.* New York: Simon & Schuster, 1984.

Felker, Clay. *Casey Stengel's Secret.* New York: Walker, 1961.

Graham, Frank. *Casey Stengel: His Half-Century* in *Baseball.* New York: Day, 1958.

Kahn, Roger. *The Era 1947–1957: When the Yankees, the Giants, and the Dodgers Ruled the World.* New York: Ticknor & Fields, 1993.

MacLean, Norman. *Casey Stengel: A Biography.* New York: Drake, 1976.

INDEX

PICTURE CREDITS
National Baseball Library and Archive, Cooperstown, NY: pp. 11, 14, 18, 20, 24, 60; UPI/Bettmann: pp. 2, 8–9, 13, 25, 26, 28, 31, 32, 34, 36, 38, 40, 44, 47, 48, 50, 53, 56, 58.

LOIS P. NICHOLSON holds a bachelor of science degree in elementary education and a master's degree in education from Salisbury State University. She has worked as a school librarian in both elementary and middle schools in Rock Hill, Maryland. She has also written *Cal Ripken, Jr.: Quiet Hero* (Tidewater, 1993) and biographies of George Washington Carver, Michael Jackson, and Oprah Winfrey for Chelsea House.

JIM MURRAY, veteran sports columnist of the *Los Angeles Times,* is one of America's most acclaimed writers. He has been named "America's Best Sportswriter" by the National Association of Sportscasters and Sportswriters 14 times, was awarded the Red Smith Award, and was twice winner of the National Headliner Award. In addition, he was awarded the J. Taylor Spink Award in 1987 for "meritorious contributions to baseball writing." With this award came his 1988 induction into the National Baseball Hall of Fame in Cooperstown, New York. In 1990, Jim Murray was awarded the Pulitzer Prize for Commentary.

EARL WEAVER is the winningest manager in Baltimore Orioles history by a wide margin. He compiled 1,480 victories in his 17 years at the helm. After managing eight different minor league teams, he was given the chance to lead the Orioles in 1968. Under his leadership the Orioles finished lower than second place in the American League East only four times in 17 years. One of only 12 managers in big league history to have managed in four or more World Series, Earl was named Manager of the Year in 1979. The popular Weaver had his number 5 retired in 1982, joining Brooks Robinson, Frank Robinson, and Jim Palmer, whose numbers were retired previously. Earl Weaver continues his association with the professional baseball scene by writing, broadcasting, and coaching.